THE REFUGEE
CRISIS

BY DUCHESS HARRIS, JD, PHD WITH ELISABETH HERSCHBACH

Essential Library

An Imprint of Abdo Publishing | abdobooks.com

abdobooks.com

Published by Abdo Publishing, a division of ABDO, PO Box 398166, Minneapolis, Minnesota 55439. Copyright © 2019 by Abdo Consulting Group, Inc. International copyrights reserved in all countries. No part of this book may be reproduced in any form without written permission from the publisher. Essential Library™ is a trademark and logo of Abdo Publishing.

Printed in the United States of America, North Mankato, Minnesota
082018
012019

Cover Photo: Dar Yasin/AP Images
Interior Photos: Olmo Calvo/AP Images, 4–5; Shutterstock Images, 10, 33, 79; Sk Hasan Ali/Shutterstock Images, 12; Hussein Malia/AP Images, 14–15; Sameer Al-Doumy/Contributor/AFP/Getty Images, 17; Fotosearch/Stringer/Archive Photos/Getty Images, 22; AP Images, 24, 47; Melih Cevdet Teksen/Shutterstock Images, 26–27; Christophe Ena/AP Images, 29; Ryan Remiorz/The Canadian Press/AP Images, 31; Sputnik/AP Images, 36; Red Line Editorial, 39, 63; Luiz Rampelotto/EuropaNewswire/Sipa USA via AP/AP Images, 40–41; Dar Yasin/AP Images, 50–51; STR/AP Images, 52; Hadi Mizban/AP Images, 56; Socrates Baltagiannis/picture-alliance/dpa/AP Images, 64–65; Petros Giannakouris/AP Images, 66; Andras Nagy/AP Images, 71; Henry Wasswa/picture-alliance/dpa/AP Images, 75; Kay Nietfeld/picture-alliance/dpa/AP Images, 77, 98; Alex Milan Tracy/Sipa USA via AP/AP Images, 80–81; Scott Olson/Staff/Getty Images News/Getty Images, 82; Andrew Harnik/AP Images, 88; Elaine Thompson/AP Images, 90–91; Evan Vucci/AP Images, 96

Editor: Alyssa Krekelberg
Series Designer: Maggie Villaume

Library of Congress Control Number: 2018948243

Publisher's Cataloging-in-Publication Data

Names: Harris, Duchess, author. | Herschbach, Elisabeth, author.
Title: The refugee crisis / by Duchess Harris and Elisabeth Herschbach.
Description: Minneapolis, Minnesota : Abdo Publishing, 2019 | Series: Special
     reports set 4 | Includes online resources and index.
Identifiers: ISBN 9781532116810 (lib. bdg.) | ISBN 9781532159657 (ebook)
Subjects: LCSH: Refugees--Juvenile literature. | Refugees--Legal status, laws, etc--
     Juvenile literature. | Refugees--Government policy--United States--Juvenile
     literature. | Emigration and immigration--Juvenile literature.
Classification: DDC 341.486--dc23

CONTENTS

CHAPTER ONE

DESPERATE
JOURNEYS

Late at night on April 18, 2015, the Italian coast guard received a distress call from a fishing trawler not far from the coast of Libya, a country in North Africa. It was trying to cross the choppy seas of the Mediterranean into Europe. The rickety, overcrowded vessel had already been at sea for 18 hours when it began to tilt to the side. It was packed beyond its capacity with hundreds of smuggled passengers. They came from a range of different countries, including Bangladesh, Senegal, Mali, Gambia, Eritrea, Sudan, Somalia, and Syria. Some were economic migrants, escaping poverty and hunger back home. Many others were refugees, fleeing war, violence, human rights

Many refugees travel over treacherous waters in small boats to reach safe shores.

MORE TO THE
STORY

MIGRANTS VS. REFUGEES

In a general sense, the term *migrant* refers to any person who moves between countries. However, the term is often used to refer to people who choose to move to another country, usually for financial reasons. In this sense of the term, migrants are distinct from refugees. While migrants choose to emigrate, refugees are forced out of their homelands because of violence or persecution. And unlike refugees, migrants are not recognized as having the same right to protection under international law.

However, in practice the distinction between migrants and refugees is not always clear-cut. For example, Libya was once a stable and lucrative place to work. Many West Africans moved there to seek economic opportunities. However, in 2011, war broke out. The country became extremely dangerous for migrants. They face horrific conditions, including abuse, torture, rape, kidnapping, and exploitation. Many are harassed, beaten, killed, or forced into slave labor. Because returning back home across the desert is very costly and dangerous, many migrants see fleeing to Europe as their only option. However, once they arrive in Europe they are unlikely to be granted asylum because they are seen as economic migrants and not genuine refugees.

abuses, or persecution. They hoped to find a safe haven in Europe.

The Italian coast guard radioed to the closest ship available to help, a Portuguese cargo ship. But as the cargo ship approached to help, the inexperienced captain of the smuggler's vessel lost control and rammed into the cargo ship. The fishing trawler sank. Hundreds of passengers were locked belowdecks on the trawler, unable to escape. At least 800 people died from drowning, according to official estimates. Some of the victims were children as young as 10 and 12. In total, there were only 28 known survivors. The United Nations High Commissioner for Refugees (UNHCR) called it "the deadliest incident in the Mediterranean we have ever recorded."[1]

A RECURRING TRAGEDY

The tragic shipwreck was front-page news around the

"I THOUGHT IF I STAYED IN THE COUNTRY, I WOULD BE KILLED. SO I DECIDED TO LEAVE BY BOAT. . . . WE HAD FOOD AND WATER FOR THE FIRST 15 DAYS. THEN WE DRANK SEA WATER AND TRIED TO CATCH FISH. STILL, TWO MEN DIED AND THEIR BODIES WERE THROWN INTO THE SEA. . . . NO ONE EXPECTED TO REACH SHORE, WE THOUGHT WE WOULD ALL DIE. . . . I DON'T REGRET COMING BECAUSE IN SRI LANKA, MY LIFE WAS ALSO IN DANGER."[2]

—SIVA, A 24-YEAR-OLD REFUGEE FROM SRI LANKA

world. International leaders expressed their shock and alarm. "The reality is stark and our actions must therefore be bold," European Commission president Jean-Claude Juncker said, adding, "These are human lives at stake, and the European Union [EU] as a whole has a moral and humanitarian obligation to act."[3] The EU is an economic and political union of some European countries. Pope Francis called for compassion and decisive action. "They are men and women like us, our brothers seeking a better life, starving, persecuted, wounded, exploited, victims of war," he said. "I make a heartfelt appeal to the international community to react decisively and quickly to see to it that such tragedies are not repeated."[4]

By the end of 2015, more than 3,770 people had drowned in the Mediterranean Sea while trying to make it to the safety of Europe. At least another 800 died while crossing the Aegean Sea from Turkey to Greece.[5] And more than 300 people died that same year in the Bay of Bengal in Southeast Asia, fleeing discrimination and violence in Myanmar.[7]

FATAL CROSSINGS

In addition to the deaths at sea, hundreds of refugees and migrants perish every year journeying over land. Some suffocate in the cargo compartments of trucks, stowed away by smugglers who promise them a safe passage across borders. Some fall victim to criminal gangs and armed militias along the way.

In addition, between 2014 and 2016, more than 1,200 people lost their lives in the Sahara Desert.[8] In 2017 alone, more than 400 people died trying to cross harsh desert terrain along the US–Mexico

"AN EARTHLY HELL"

Of the estimated 850 passengers on board the fishing trawler that sank on April 18, 2015, some 350 were from Eritrea.[9] This small country in the Horn of Africa has one of the world's worst human rights records. The authoritarian government severely limits citizens' religious freedom and political rights. Citizens face arbitrary arrest and torture. A system of forced conscription means that people face mandatory military service that lasts indefinitely. The United Nations (UN) refugee agency estimates that 5,000 people flee Eritrea every month.[10] The country has a total population of only around six million. Eritrea has a higher ratio of departing refugees to citizens than any other country in the world. "Eritrea has become an earthly hell, an earthly inferno for its people—and that's why they are taking such huge risks to their personal lives to escape the situation. It's because it's become unlivable," explains Welde Giorgis, who fled the country in 2006.[11]

border.[12] Many of them were escaping skyrocketing violence in El Salvador, Honduras, and Guatemala. These three countries make up Central America's Northern Triangle region, which some people consider to be one of the most dangerous regions in the world. In total, more than 60,000 people around the world died trying to make it to another country between 1996 and 2016, according to the International Organization for Migration, an organization that works to promote effective migration.[13]

FLEEING FOR LIFE

Despite the high risk of death, millions of people around the globe flee their homes every year, embarking on difficult journeys in search of safety

VIOLENCE IN CENTRAL AMERICA'S NORTHERN TRIANGLE

The countries of Central America's Northern Triangle region are not at war. However, they face a deadly epidemic of organized crime and violent gang activity. Kidnappings, rapes, and murders have become an everyday reality in communities terrorized by ruthless gangs called *maras*. The surge in violence has pushed increasing numbers of asylum seekers to flee north to Mexico or the United States in recent years. In 2010, 8,052 people from El Salvador, Honduras, and Guatemala filed asylum applications. In 2015, the number was 56,097—a staggering increase of more than 597 percent in just five years.[14] One of these asylum seekers is Rosa, a single mother from Honduras. Her older son was murdered after he refused to join a gang. When her younger son began receiving death threats, Rosa knew they had to flee for their lives. She and her remaining son and daughter escaped to Mexico, where they have applied for asylum.

Many refugees, including children, face harsh conditions as they search for a safe home.

and a better life. Refugees leave everything behind—their homes, their countries, and most of their belongings. Some refugees end up separated from their families, possibly never to see them again. Many hand their entire life savings over to smugglers or go into massive debt to pay for an escape from their country. Along the way, refugees may face exploitation and abuse by smugglers, armed criminals, and corrupt border-control officials. Refugees may get caught up in violence and conflict passing through war-torn countries.

Many of those people who do make it out safely end up stuck in refugee camps and detention centers for many months or even years. The conditions inside many of

Even when refugees approach a country where they hope to find sanctuary, many people are held at the border before they can enter.

these camps are so bad that the international medical-aid organization Doctors Without Borders has described them as "on the brink of a humanitarian emergency."[15]

Refugees undertake all these risks because of a tragic reality—the dangers of staying put are even greater. As the UNHCR puts it, "Refugees have to move if they are to save their lives or preserve their freedom. . . . If other countries do not let them in, and do not help them once they are in, then they may be condemning them to death—or to an intolerable life in the shadows, without sustenance and without rights."[16]

COUNTING THE DEAD

Accurately estimating refugee and migrant deaths is difficult. Official body counts are based only on the deaths that are recorded. But many die in remote areas and their bodies are never found. This means that the real death toll is almost certainly much higher than the estimates. In fact, some experts calculate that for every dead body that is found, at least another two go undiscovered. Many of the dead bodies that are recovered remain unidentified. Many refugees are forced to flee without identifying documents. In other cases, the documents are lost or stolen along the way. Sometimes, bodies are too badly damaged to identify. For example, in 2013, 387 migrants and refugees drowned off the coast of the Italian island of Lampedusa. Less than one-half of the victims have been officially identified.[17] This means that countless families are left in the dark about the fate of their missing loved ones.

CHAPTER TWO

PROTECTING
REFUGEES

The term *refugee* dates back to the 1600s, when it was first used to refer to the Huguenots—a group of Protestants who fled France because of religious persecution. Today's refugees come from many different countries and flee for a range of different reasons. However, like the Huguenots in the 1600s, they face the same basic plight: they are forced to seek protection in another country because their own has become too dangerous for them.

In 2005, Andre Twendele escaped from the Democratic Republic of the Congo, a country in central Africa. He escaped after he was beaten, arrested, and sentenced to death by firing squad for helping organize a student protest against the country's authoritarian

Sometimes there's not enough food to feed everyone in refugee camps.

president, Joseph Kabila. He spent 11 years in a refugee camp in Malawi, a country in East Africa, before being granted a visa to resettle in the United States.

Zorina Khatun faced ethnic and religious discrimination in Burma, her home country in Asia, for being Rohingya—a persecuted Muslim minority in the Buddhist-majority nation. She sought safety in Bangladesh after soldiers stormed her village in a brutal military crackdown in 2017. Many villagers were arrested and beaten. The soldiers set everything on fire, and many people were burned alive. Others were shot dead, including Khatun's 25-year-old brother.

George Mukhwezi faced a different kind of persecution in his home country of Uganda, a country in East Africa. The persecution against him was based on his sexual orientation. Being gay is illegal in Uganda, and lesbian, gay, bisexual, transgender, and queer (LGBTQ) people suffer from rampant discrimination and violence. "My life was in danger when people and the police realized I was gay,"

Destruction and violence in Syria cause many people to flee.

Mukhwezi explained. "I decided to escape and save my life. Uganda is a dangerous country for LGBT people like me."[2] He took refuge in Kenya, a country in East Africa, where being gay is also illegal but treated with more tolerance.

THE RIGHT TO ASYLUM

When refugees like Twendele, Khatun, and Mukhwezi seek protection in another country, this is known as seeking asylum. Although *asylum seeker* and *refugee* are related terms, they have slightly different meanings. An asylum seeker is someone who claims asylum, or protection, in another country but whose status as a refugee has not yet been determined. A refugee is someone who has been granted refugee status and so is entitled to special

LEGAL LINGO

As with any legal field, refugee law has its share of technical terms. There are a few key terms used in refugee contexts. The first is *asylum*, or the protection one country gives to refugees from another country. Another term is *deportation*, or the act of sending people back to their own country or to another country against their will. *Non-refoulement* refers to the right of refugees not to be returned against their will to a country where their lives or freedoms would be threatened. Another term is *quota*, or the number of immigrants, refugees, or asylum seekers a country lets in under its immigration policies. *Repatriation* is returning a person to his or her home country, and *resettlement* is the transfer of refugees from a country where they are being given asylum to another country where they will be allowed to permanently resettle.

protections under international law. Asylum seekers gain refugee status once the country where they have applied for asylum reviews their case and determines that they would be in danger if they returned home.

The concept of asylum has ancient roots. The ancient Egyptians, Hebrews, and Greeks designated temples and sacred places as protected spaces where the persecuted could take refuge. Many of the world's major religions also include a tradition of offering sanctuary, or a safe haven, to those under pursuit. However, the laws and practices used to determine refugee status are much more recent. It was not until after World War II (1939–1945) that the current international framework for refugee protections was established.

A WORLD AT WAR

World War II was the most devastating conflict in human history. More than 60 million people died. As many as two-thirds of those who died were civilians.[3] Up to six million Jews were rounded up and massacred under the Nazi regime led by dictator Adolf Hitler.[4] Several million others were also murdered, including gypsies, LGBTQ people, people involved in Jehovah's Witnesses, and people with disabilities.

However, even as Nazi atrocities escalated, Western leaders were slow to respond. On the eve of the war, delegates from dozens of nations, including the United States, held a meeting in the French resort town of Evian. The

TURNING AMERICA'S BACK

Even as Nazi attacks against Jews became headline news in the United States, public opinion remained firmly against raising quotas to let in more refugees. This anti-refugee bias was fueled by paranoia that the refugees were secretly spies and were therefore a national security threat. Fears that refugees would take away US jobs also played a role. In polls of the day, two-thirds of Americans agreed that the United States should keep Jewish refugees out. Two-thirds were even against letting in 10,000 Jewish refugee children.[5] This anti-refugee bias took a deadly turn in the case of the SS *St. Louis*, an ocean liner carrying more than 900 Jewish refugees hoping to dock off the coast of Florida. The United States turned the boat away and the refugees were sent back to Europe. A quarter of the passengers later died in Nazi death camps.[6]

purpose was to decide whether to provide a safe haven to the rising tide of Jewish refugees fleeing Hitler's Germany. One by one, the delegates offered their excuses. Not a single Western leader agreed to take in more Jewish refugees. Only one country agreed to open its doors: the tiny island nation of the Dominican Republic.

In the United States, physicist Albert Einstein lamented to First Lady Eleanor Roosevelt that a "wall of bureaucratic measures" made it "all but impossible to give refuge in America to many worthy persons who are the victims of . . . cruelty in Europe."[7] Strict immigration quotas, enacted in 1924, limited the number of immigrants who could be admitted into the United States. Public opposition meant that there was no political will to raise the

EINSTEIN'S HUMANITARIAN LEGACY

Albert Einstein's scientific legacy makes him a household name. His personal history as a refugee is less well known. When the Nazis rose to power in his home country of Germany, Einstein, who was Jewish, found it increasingly difficult to work. He was persecuted by the Nazi regime. His books were burned. He was even accused of treason. In 1932, Einstein escaped to the United States as a refugee, where he was offered a position at Princeton University. However, he was troubled by the tragic plight of other Jews stuck in Nazi Germany. As a result, he devoted himself to helping those suffering back home under Hitler and championing the cause of refugees. He also helped to found the International Rescue Committee (IRC), an international humanitarian-aid organization.

quota—even for refugees fleeing Nazi atrocities. In 1939 and again in 1940, even a bill to let in refugee children failed in Congress.

LEARNING FROM HISTORY

By the time the war ended in 1945, cities across Europe lay in ruins. Millions of refugees had been displaced from their homes by war. By 1947, some people were still waiting in resettlement camps that held displaced people. Western leaders woke up to the realization that they could not afford to repeat their mistakes when it came to refugees.

The horrors of World War II inspired an international effort to protect human rights, including the rights of refugees. This effort began with the 1945 founding of the United Nations (UN), an intergovernmental organization that aims to promote international peace and justice. Over the next few years, the UN drafted several important international human rights documents, including the Universal Declaration of Human Rights (UDHR) and the 1951 Convention Relating to the Status of Refugees, known in short as the 1951 Refugee Convention.

Former first lady Eleanor Roosevelt was part of the UDHR drafting committee.

HUMAN RIGHTS MILESTONES

The UDHR, adopted in 1948, outlines fundamental human rights to which all people are entitled. These include the right of all persons to seek asylum from persecution in other countries. The 1951 Refugee Convention provided the first general definition of a refugee for the purposes of international law. According to this definition, refugees and asylum seekers are people who are outside of their country of origin and unwilling to return home because of a well-founded fear of persecution based on race, religion, nationality, political opinion, or membership in a particular social group.

In addition, the 1951 Refugee Convention established a legal basis for the international protection of refugees. It outlines certain basic rights and minimum standards of treatment to which refugees are entitled. For example, refugees should be allowed freedom of religion, freedom of movement, the right to work, and access to schools and courts. The convention also established basic legal rights for refugees that countries are expected to respect. These include the right to seek asylum and the right not to be sent back to a country where one's well-being, freedom, or life would be at serious risk. Significantly, the convention recognizes that desperate circumstances can force refugees to violate immigration rules. Thus, it states that refugees should not be penalized for illegally entering or staying in another country.

EXPANDING THE SCOPE OF REFUGEE PROTECTIONS

The 1951 Refugee Convention is the "centerpiece of international refugee protection today," as the UNHCR puts it.[8] However, it was originally drafted to serve a narrow purpose: to tackle the refugee crisis created by

World War II. As such, the original convention had a limited scope. It applied only to refugees in Europe displaced before 1951. And it was intended to be temporary— staying in effect only until people were able to return to their homes.

However, long after the end of World War II, new conflicts creating new flows of refugees continued to crop up around the globe, not just in Europe. For example, in 1948, the Arab-Israeli War created an estimated 700,000 Palestinian refugees.[9] Hundreds of thousands of Algerians escaped to Tunisia and Morocco—countries in North Africa—between 1954 and 1962, fleeing civil war in

The Soviet Union invaded Hungary to stop the Hungarian Revolution in 1956.

Algeria. And some 200,000 Hungarians fled over their borders to Austria and Yugoslavia when the Soviet Union's tanks rolled into Budapest, Hungary, in 1956.[10]

It was clear that the 1951 Refugee Convention's mandate needed to be expanded. This happened in 1967, when the Protocol Relating to the Status of Refugees was ratified. The 1967 Protocol removed all geographical and chronological limitations, making the 1951 Refugee Convention universal in scope. In addition, evolving legal standards and regional treaties addressing the rights of refugees have broadened and supplemented refugee policies across the globe.

As of 2015, 148 countries had signed either the 1951 Refugee Convention or the 1967 Protocol, while 142 countries were signatories to both.[11] The United States signed only the 1967 Protocol. In addition, many countries are signatories to regional agreements and declarations governing refugee protection.

CHAPTER THREE

A HUMANITARIAN
EMERGENCY
IN SYRIA

T he second half of the 1900s brought many large-scale refugee crises. Starting in the 1970s, millions of Vietnamese people were displaced from South Vietnam to North Vietnam. An estimated ten million Bengalis escaped to India during the 1971 Bangladesh War of Independence. More than six million Afghan refugees were forced out of their country by a Soviet invasion in 1979. And some two million Rwandans fled to neighboring countries during the 1994 Rwandan genocide.[1]

Many children are displaced from areas such as Syria. The United Nations International Children's Emergency Fund calls the situation a child refugee crisis.

However, the modern world is witnessing greater numbers of people displaced by conflict and persecution than at any other time since World War II. These record-high numbers of refugees and other displaced people are the result of increasingly devastating violent conflicts occurring around the world. The deadliest of these conflicts is the civil war in Syria—the single largest source of refugees worldwide today.

FROM PEACEFUL PROTESTS TO CIVIL WAR

Syria's civil war has killed hundreds of thousands of Syrians and driven more than one-half of the population from their homes. The UNHCR calls it the "most dramatic humanitarian crisis the world has faced in a very long time."[2]

The crisis began with a peaceful act of dissent by a group of schoolboys in a town in southern Syria. In March 2011, the teenagers spray-painted prodemocratic slogans across a school wall. In response, the teens were arrested and tortured. People were outraged by this brutal treatment. There was also broader discontent about life under the dictatorship of Syrian president Bashar al-Assad.

Police threw tear gas at Tunisian protesters in 2011 during the Arab Spring.

Demonstrations broke out across the country. These protests were inspired by a movement known as the Arab Spring—a wave of prodemocratic protests against authoritarian governments across the Arab world that began in 2010.

Assad's regime responded with brutal force. Government security forces opened fire on demonstrators, killing many. This triggered even greater unrest. Hundreds of thousands of people took to the streets nationwide, demanding Assad's resignation. But as protests intensified, so did the government's crackdown. Opponents formed rebel armies to take on Assad. Soon, the situation escalated into a full-blown war.

CIVILIANS CAUGHT IN THE CROSS FIRE

Over the course of the conflict, both government forces and armed opposition groups have committed war crimes and human rights abuses. Assad has used chemical weapons and conducted indiscriminate bombings against civilians. Thousands of people have been tortured, jailed, and executed for opposing Assad's regime. Rebel groups have also deliberately targeted civilians and have been accused of torturing people, taking hostages, and committing mass killings.

In the chaos of war, extremist groups have been able to flourish. The most prominent of these is the Islamic State in Iraq and Syria, often

WINTER ARRIVES

The so-called Arab Spring began in the North African country of Tunisia on December 17, 2010, when a street vendor named Mohamed Bouazizi set himself on fire. His desperate act was a protest against officials who had confiscated his wares and harassed him because he refused to pay a bribe. Bouazizi's death inspired mass demonstrations across the country by people fed up with high levels of unemployment and corruption and a lack of political freedoms. As the protests intensified, Tunisian president Zine El-Abidine Ben Ali was forced to resign. He fled to Saudi Arabia, ending his 23-year reign. Similar prodemocratic uprisings also broke out in other Middle Eastern countries, including Egypt, Libya, Bahrain, and Yemen. However, the initial promise of the Arab Spring soon faded as peaceful protests were crushed by bloodshed, civil war, and a resurgence of repressive authoritarian regimes across the region. This was a turn of events that political commentators refer to as the Arab Winter.

known as ISIS. This group uses terror tactics to impose its harsh fundamentalist interpretation of Islam on people under its control. Those who violate its strict religious laws are subjected to severe punishments, including public executions, amputations, and lashings. Women and religious minorities are treated especially harshly.

By 2014, ISIS had won control over large parts of Syria. In the process, ISIS fighters were responsible for many atrocities, including massacres, decapitations, and deadly attacks on civilians. As of 2018, ISIS had largely been driven out of the areas it had seized. However, the terror group's brutal tactics left lasting scars on the war-torn country, and experts warn of a possible resurgence.

Troops in the Middle East fight to hold their ground against ISIS.

A COUNTRY IN RUINS

The ongoing violence has devastated the country. By
2018, more than 400,000 people had been killed. At
least 25 percent of those casualties have been civilians,
including children.[3] Attacks and bombardments by
government and opposition forces are responsible for the
majority of these deaths. However, air strikes by Russia and
the United States have added to the death toll. Since 2014,
a United States–led coalition has carried out air strikes
against ISIS and provided support to rebel groups trying
to overthrow Assad. Since 2015, Russia has conducted
aerial bombings and provided ground support to help
Assad and the Syrian government's forces. According to
the UN, both countries have been responsible for many
civilian deaths.

As Brookings Institution researchers Elizabeth Ferris
and Kemal Kirişci explain, "It is difficult to overestimate the
impact of the war on normal life in Syria."[4] Eighty percent
of Syrians have been reduced to living in poverty. Average
life expectancy has plummeted by 20 years. One-half
of all children are out of school.[5] In addition, countless

Some US-led air strikes in Syria have targeted ISIS fighters.

buildings have been reduced to rubble, including many schools, hospitals, and public utilities. In some cases, entire neighborhoods and towns have been leveled.

Bombs have also destroyed farms and crops, creating a food crisis. As a result, more than three million children under the age of five don't have enough to eat. An estimated 13.5 million people—more than one-half of the population—are in need of humanitarian assistance.[6] Yet Syrian authorities routinely block humanitarian aid convoys from distributing food and supplies.

"WE CANNOT BEAR ANY MORE OF THIS"

The desperate situation in Syria has driven millions of people from their homes. As of April 2018, more than five

REFUGEES VS. IDPs

Crossing an international border is a requirement for being considered a refugee. Because internally displaced people (IDPs) have not crossed into another country, they are not considered refugees. This means that they are not guaranteed the same rights under international law. However, IDPs face many of the same challenges and risks as refugees. Like refugees, they are fleeing violence, war, persecution, or human rights abuses. In fact, in many cases, IDPs are more vulnerable because they stay closer to the danger zone. And as Elizabeth Rushing of the Norwegian Refugee Council says, IDPs often become "tomorrow's refugees."[9] According to Rushing, many refugees first try to find safety by moving within their own country before undertaking the risks and dangers of a journey abroad. For example, the Mardini family fled to Europe from Syria in 2015, sailing to the Greek island of Lesbos from Turkey. First, however, they were internally displaced within Syria twice, moving from one town to another to escape bombardment.

million Syrian refugees had fled the country. Another six million or more were internally displaced.[7] This means that they were displaced from their homes but were still within the borders of their own country. Roughly one-half of the refugees pouring out of Syria are children, including four-year-old Shahad. Before the war, Shahad's family lived a happy life in a village near the city of Hama in western Syria. However, in 2012, her village was bombed. Her family's three-story home was leveled. Seven members of her family were killed, including her baby sister and ten-year-old brother.[8] Shahad was pulled from the rubble with gashes on her face. She and the surviving members of her family fled over the border to Lebanon with nothing but a single suitcase.

But although Shahad and millions of other Syrians have fled the escalating violence, many others have been trapped in place, unable to escape. For example, in Syria's Eastern Ghouta region, both government and opposition forces have made it difficult for civilians to leave. The area's roughly 390,000 residents have been under almost constant siege by government forces and their allies since 2013. In a single four-day period in February 2018, the area, which opposition forces were in, was hit by 420 air strikes and 140 barrel bombs. These deadly bombs are filled with explosives and shrapnel. They are designed to shatter into thousands of fragments upon impact, obliterating whatever they hit. In the two-week period from February 18 to March 4, 2018, more than 1,000 people were killed and 3,900 wounded in Eastern Ghouta.[10]

"People are trapped in the middle between the advancement and bombardment of the forces of the regime and its allies, and the armed groups on ground," a team of doctors explained in an open letter to the UN.[11] The bombardment is so severe that many people are too

afraid to go outside. Those who do try to leave the area are often stopped at checkpoints by armed rebels who block them from leaving. In other cases, government security forces turn people back, preventing them from fleeing to safe zones.

With no safe way out, many residents of Eastern Ghouta are forced to shelter underground, hoping to stay safe from the relentless bombings. For example, Asia is a 28-year-old mother who lives with her three children in a basement underneath a half-destroyed house. Her husband was killed while he was on his way to work. "My daughter is sick. Her hair is falling out because she is so afraid," she told the British Broadcasting Corporation. "I hope that we can leave Eastern Ghouta because we cannot bear any more of this."[12]

Oftentimes, refugees can take only what they can carry when fleeing a country.

FROM THE
HEADLINES

A WAR ON MANY FRONTS

One of the reasons that the Syrian conflict has been so hard to resolve is that there are many factions involved in the fight. There are hundreds of different opposition groups in Syria. In some cases, these rebel groups are fighting not just Assad but also each other. Many of them are small groups operating on a local level. Others have joined together to form large, powerful alliances, such as the Free Syrian Army and the Syrian Democratic Forces. A host of foreign powers have also gotten involved, backing different sides in the conflict. Russia, Iran, and Hezbollah, a militant group based in Lebanon, are on the side of the Syrian government. The United States, Saudi Arabia, Iran, and Turkey support various rebel groups. At the same time, the United States, Russia, the Syrian government, and the opposition forces are all separately battling ISIS. The Kurds, an ethnic minority in the region, add another dimension to the conflict. They are battling ISIS but are also trying to set up their own independent territory. Even though they are fighting a common enemy—ISIS—Turkey has bombed the Kurdish rebels to stop their advance. Turkey views the Syrian Kurds as an extension of a rebel group that has been fighting for an independent Kurdish state within Turkey for decades.

The conflict in Syria is complicated in part because of the different groups involved.

PLAYERS IN THE
SYRIAN CONFLICT

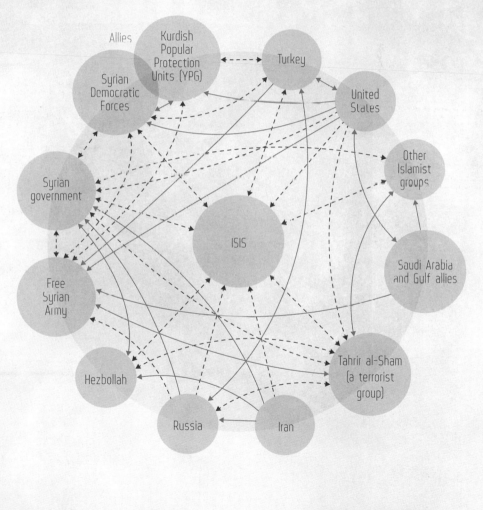

CHAPTER FOUR

GLOBAL
CONFLICT

U NHCR head Filippo Grandi has called the situation in Syria "the biggest humanitarian and refugee crisis of our time, a continuing cause of suffering for millions which should be garnering a groundswell of support around the world."[1] But while Syria is the biggest source of refugees today, it is far from the only one.

Around the world, new wars and violent conflicts are pushing increasingly large numbers of refugees out of their homes. This surge in conflict worldwide is creating a global crisis of displacement that is testing the international community's ability to respond. David Miliband, chief executive officer (CEO) of the humanitarian aid group International Rescue

Filippo Grandi was elected as the UN high commissioner for refugees in 2016.

> "THE SUFFERING OF THE SOUTH SUDANESE PEOPLE IS JUST UNIMAGINABLE. THEY ARE CLOSE TO THE ABYSS. VIOLENCE IS AT THE ROOT OF THIS CRISIS. . . . MANY ARE DYING FROM HUNGER AND DISEASE, MANY MORE HAVE FLED THEIR HOMELAND FOR SAFETY ABROAD."[5]
>
> **—DAVID BEASLEY, THE EXECUTIVE DIRECTOR OF THE UN WORLD FOOD PROGRAMME**

Committee (IRC), says, "The rising tide of people forced to leave their homes because of conflict or persecution is one of the most challenging issues facing the world today."[2]

VIOLENCE ON THE RISE

Violent conflict in Ukraine has caused an estimated 1.4 million refugees to flee the eastern European nation since 2014. Another 1.7 million people have been internally displaced. Civil war broke out after Russia annexed Crimea, a Ukrainian territory, in 2014.[3] This fueled a deadly conflict between government forces and Russia-backed separatists. As of 2017, some 10,000 people, including 3,000 civilians, had been killed.[4]

Civil war has also uprooted civilians in the new nation of South Sudan. The east-central African nation became independent from Sudan in 2011. Yet only two years later, fighting broke out between government and opposition groups battling for political control. Since then, the impoverished nation has descended into brutal civil war, forcing more than one million South Sudanese to flee to neighboring countries, including Uganda and Sudan. Much of the country's escalating violence occurs along ethnic lines between two tribes, the Dinka and the Nuer. The vast majority of refugees are women and children.

In northern Nigeria, the radical Islamist terrorist group Boko Haram has killed tens of thousands of people since 2009, terrorizing civilians with a lethal campaign of suicide bombings, kidnappings, armed assaults, and systematic human rights abuses. Ongoing clashes between the Nigerian military and Boko Haram have also put civilians in harm's way. From 2013 to 2015, more than two million people had been driven from their homes. A quarter million fled to the neighboring countries of Cameroon, Chad, and Niger to escape deadly raids and attacks.[6]

In Yemen, armed conflict has forced more than two million civilians to flee their homes. Rebel forces ousted the internationally recognized president in 2015. In response, a Saudi-led coalition supporting the exiled president began an ongoing campaign of crippling air strikes to crush the rebellion. More than 15,000 people

> "THE WAR KILLED OUR ONLY INCOME, WHICH WAS WORKING AS A FISHERMAN, AND NOW WE ARE JOBLESS AND HOPELESS. . . . THE BOATS THAT WE WERE WORKING ON WERE BOMBED. NOW MY FAMILY AND I DON'T HAVE ENOUGH TO EAT."[10]
>
> **—TAIE AL-NAHARI, 53-YEAR-OLD YEMENI**

have been killed in the escalating violence.[7] At the same time, Saudi Arabian blockades on Yemen's key ports have cut off the flow of essential goods into the country, including lifesaving medicines, food, and fuel.

The result is a full-blown humanitarian crisis. According to UN estimates, as many as 18 million Yemenis are facing food shortages. More than eight million of those people are at immediate risk of starvation. That includes almost two million children who are severely malnourished.[8] "Either we die from the bombing or from the hunger," one Yemeni grandmother said.[9] Her family lost its livelihood in the war. Her two grandchildren are sick, but the family has no money to buy food or medicine.

MORE WARS, DEADLIER WARS, AND LONGER WARS

Syria, Ukraine, South Sudan, Nigeria, and Yemen were only a few of the major political hot spots in 2018. There were also armed conflicts, violent uprisings, or situations of civil unrest going on in Afghanistan, Iraq, Libya, Somalia, Burundi, the Central African Republic, Mali, the Democratic Republic of the Congo, Burma, Ethiopia, Eritrea, and parts of Turkey, among other places. The average number of civil wars taking place around the world has increased tenfold since 1990. Since 2007, there has been an almost threefold increase in major civil wars. According to researchers at the United Nations University in Tokyo, Japan, these wars have also been growing increasingly deadly. Battle deaths have increased sixfold since 2011, and violence against civilians is on the rise.

But wars are not only breaking out more frequently and becoming deadlier. Many

A VICIOUS CYCLE

Even before the outbreak of war, Yemen was the Middle East's poorest country. Two years into the war, UN officials warned that the humanitarian situation in the country was becoming "catastrophic and rapidly deteriorating."[11] This vicious cycle of war and poverty is all too common. Poor countries are more likely to be unstable and conflict ridden. In turn, war deepens poverty and worsens preexisting social and economic problems. For example, in Nigeria, violent attacks by Boko Haram have devastated a region already ravaged by droughts, floods, and extreme poverty. The violence has brought trade and business activity to a standstill in some areas. Farmers are unable to tend their fields. "Malnutrition and disease outbreaks hover at emergency levels. Some 5.5 million people do not have enough to eat," UN official Stephen O'Brien says. "The emergence of Boko Haram has pushed them over the edge."[12]

of the world's conflicts are also lasting longer or relapsing sooner. Since the 1960s, the relapse rate of conflicts has steadily increased. In the early 2000s, 60 percent of conflicts relapsed within five years.[13] Many other conflicts drag on for years with no resolution in sight. For example, Syria and Libya have been in the grip of civil war since 2011, without any sign of letup. War in Somalia has raged since 1991. The Democratic Republic of the Congo has yet to recover from the 1997–2003 conflict that killed millions of people. And the violence in South Sudan comes on the heels of more than two decades of fighting in Sudan before the two countries became independent.

In some countries, one conflict has spiraled into another, creating ongoing

"BLOOD FLOWS EVERYWHERE"

A long history of violence between the Hutu and Tutsi ethnic groups has made Burundi—a country in East Africa—one of Africa's most unstable nations. The country has been scarred by two genocides: a Tutsi-led massacre of Hutus in 1972 and a Hutu-led massacre of Tutsis in 1993. A bloody 12-year civil war raged from 1994 to 2005. And in 2015, political unrest broke out again. Since then, the country has been in a state of perpetual violence. "Blood flows everywhere in Burundi, that's how things are," Thierry, a 27-year-old refugee, said.[14] Since 2015, hundreds of thousands of refugees have poured out of Burundi. One of those fleeing the violence was 80-year-old Sindatuma Elizabeth. She walked for 12 hours to reach the neighboring country of Tanzania. This was the fourth time she became a refugee. "It's sad to flee at this age," she said. "It was difficult on the way. I was weak."[15]

The United States and other Western countries were involved in the
Gulf War. The conflict started after Iraq invaded Kuwait in 1990.

waves of violence and long-term instability. In Iraq, for

example, the United States' invasion and occupation

in 2003 sparked an armed insurgency, or uprising, that

escalated into civil war in 2014. Millions of Iraqis were

displaced from their homes, fleeing violence from the

radical Islamic terrorist group ISIS. That number comes on

top of previous waves of refugees created by the Iran-Iraq

War (1980–1988) and the Gulf War (1990).

Afghanistan has an even longer history of unrest. The

war-torn nation has not seen peace since the 1970s. This

ongoing instability has created one of the world's largest

and longest-displaced refugee populations, with some

MORE TO THE
STORY

MINORITIES
UNDER ATTACK

Iraqi civilians of all backgrounds have suffered under ISIS atrocities. However, ethnic and religious minorities have been especially at risk. In 2014, ISIS mounted a brutal campaign against the Yazidis, members of a tiny ethnic and religious minority group in northern Iraq. The Yazidis practice a faith that combines elements of Islam, Christianity, and Zoroastrianism—an ancient religion with roots in Persia (modern-day Iran).

ISIS militants rounded up countless Yazidis and forced them to convert to Islam or face death. Thousands of men were massacred. Thousands of women and young girls were kidnapped, raped, tortured, and forced into sexual slavery. Nadia Murad was only 20 years old when ISIS militants captured her village in northern Iraq on August 15, 2014. Her mother and brothers were slaughtered. She was abducted and sold at a slave market. After three months of horrendous abuse, she managed to escape. She now lives in Germany, where she has been granted asylum, and she is a vocal advocate for the Yazidi community. In 2016, Murad and another Yazidi survivor, Lamiya Aji Bashar, were awarded the Sakharov Award, Europe's most prestigious human rights award, to honor that advocacy work.

three million Afghans living in the neighboring countries of Pakistan and Iran. Deadly clashes between government forces and the Taliban, an Islamic extremist movement, have displaced new waves of refugees in recent years. In 2017 alone, an average of 1,200 Afghans fled their homes each day.[16]

Fighting between government forces and the Taliban began escalating in 2015. But the United States got involved in 2001. The United States invaded Afghanistan after the September 11, 2001, terrorist attacks. The Taliban, then in power in Afghanistan, was accused of protecting Osama bin Laden and the al-Qaeda terrorists behind the September 11 attacks. The US invasion drove the Taliban from power, and a new government took over. Since then, however, the Taliban has reemerged and is waging war against the government for control of the country. Terrified civilians are caught in the middle. According to the UN, 2016 was the deadliest year on record for Afghan civilians, with 11,418 people killed or injured in attacks by armed groups.[17]

CHAPTER FIVE

THE WORLDWIDE COMMUNITY

As of 2016, 65.6 million people have been forcibly displaced because of conflict, persecution, or human rights abuses. That number includes almost 23 million refugees who have crossed into another country to reach safety. Nearly one-half of those refugees are children under the age of 18.[1]

The level of displacement worldwide has surged since 2010. According to the UNHCR, 24 people are driven from their homes every minute because of violence or persecution. By comparison, in 2005, the number was six per minute. By the end of 2016, the number of people displaced worldwide had reached

A child refugee from a camp in Bangladesh approached aid workers, asking for food.

the highest level ever recorded. In total, they account for one of every 113 people on Earth.[2] That is more people than the population of Italy.

The world's growing displacement crisis has been fueled by changing patterns of violence and conflict around the globe. Violent conflicts have spiked worldwide. These conflicts are lasting longer. And they are having an increasingly devastating effect on civilians. But although the world's growing displacement crisis is driven by conflict, it is compounded by the international community's failure to adequately deal with the problem.

AN UNEQUAL BURDEN

The drafters of the 1951 Refugee Convention recognized that protecting refugees requires international cooperation. The responsibility of tackling large-scale

The UN has peacekeepers that protect some refugee camps. One camp is in Wau, South Sudan.

displacements must be fairly shared among all countries, rather than resting disproportionately on the shoulders of a few. However, in practice, that is not what happens. The vast majority of the world's refugees are hosted by only a handful of countries. Moreover, the countries bearing the lion's share of the burden are predominantly ones with the fewest resources to spare, including some of the world's poorest countries. Many of these countries are dealing with their own humanitarian crises as well.

The same pattern holds when it comes to Syrian refugees specifically. The vast majority of Syrian refugees are living in just five neighboring Middle Eastern countries: Turkey, Lebanon, Jordan, Iraq, and Egypt. Only three of those countries—Turkey, Lebanon, and Jordan—are shouldering the bulk of the burden. As of 2016, Turkey was host to more than 2.5 million Syrian refugees—more than any other country. More than 655,000 Syrian refugees are in Jordan, representing 10 percent of the country's population. Lebanon has since taken in more than one million refugees from its war-torn neighbor.[3] The United States let in just 18,007 Syrian refugees between 2011 and 2016.[4]

STARVED FOR FUNDS

Lebanon's prime minister Saad al-Hariri has said that the massive influx of refugees has put great stress on the country. Other developing nations bearing the brunt of the refugee crisis are in the same boat. Countries with struggling economies largely depend on humanitarian assistance to cope with the needs of refugees. Yet refugee assistance programs are consistently and severely underfunded.

The UN depends entirely on voluntary donations from individual governments and private donors to finance its humanitarian programs. Year after year, these programs fall short of their funding targets. Severe funding shortfalls mean cuts in food rations and essential services such as health

FINDING SHELTER

Many of the world's refugees live in camps. These are hastily built settlements set up to respond to a sudden refugee crisis. For example, the Bidi Bidi camp in northern Uganda sprang up in 2016 to accommodate the flood of South Sudanese refugees pouring into the country. It is now Africa's biggest refugee camp, home to hundreds of thousands of refugees. Camps are intended to be temporary settlements. In reality, many refugees end up spending a great portion of their lives in them, living in makeshift huts and tents. Abdullah Mire, a 27-year-old Somali refugee, has lived in Kenya's Dadaab camp since he was three. Growing up in the camp, he faced many hardships including lack of clean water, food shortages, and crowded conditions. The family's only shelter was a plastic sheet.

care for already vulnerable refugees. In the first quarter of 2015, the UN's World Food Programme was forced to cut food assistance to Syrian refugees in Lebanon and Jordan by as much as 30 percent.[5] Burundian refugees in Rwanda, Somali and Sudanese refugees in Kenya, and millions of other refugees in overburdened developing nations have also seen their food rations slashed.

The consequences can be deadly. When food supplies ran out in the Ugandan refugee camp where Oliver Wani was sheltering, he risked returning home to his native South Sudan. Two weeks later, he was dead—a victim of the bloody conflict he had fled in the first place. His body was found alongside that of another returning refugee. The ground was strewn with bullet casings. His father said that Wani had gone to South Sudan to search for food.

Food assistance has been cut by as much as 75 percent at refugee camps hosting the million-plus refugees who have fled South Sudan's brutal war.[6]

"THE SITUATION IS GETTING DESPERATE. . . . WE ARE ALREADY SEEING CHILDREN WHO AREN'T ABLE TO GO TO SCHOOL, FAMILIES WHO CANNOT ACCESS ADEQUATE SHELTER OR PROVIDE FOR THEIR BASIC NEEDS."[7]

—UN HIGH COMMISSIONER FOR REFUGEES FILIPPO GRANDI, DESCRIBING HOW LACK OF FUNDING IS PUTTING SYRIAN REFUGEES AT RISK

Grandi notes that countries hosting many refugees will not be able to continue supporting them unless the international community helps. The main host countries for South Sudanese refugees are Uganda, Ethiopia, Kenya, Sudan, the Central African Republic, and the Democratic Republic of the Congo. All six of these countries are among the world's poorest 40 nations. The Democratic Republic of the Congo, the world's second-poorest nation, is sheltering 526,000 refugees even as it struggles with its own problems of political instability.[8]

In 2013, Syrian refugees gathered as food was distributed in a refugee camp in Iraq.

A FAILING SYSTEM

Experts say that lack of adequate international support has left poor host countries straining to cope and millions of refugees struggling to survive. "The refugee system is failing badly," note Oxford University professors Paul Collier and Alexander Betts, authors of *Refuge: Rethinking Refugee Policy in a Changing World*. "The founding statute of UNHCR outlines two main roles: to provide protection to refugees and to find long-term solutions to their plight. Yet neither is being met."[10]

The UN identifies three viable long-term solutions for refugees. They can return home when it is safe again. They can be resettled to a third country. Or they can integrate into the host country where they have sought protection. However, for the overwhelming majority of refugees, these solutions are increasingly out of reach. According to Collier and Betts, fewer refugees have access to any of these options.

TRAPPED IN LIMBO

With violent conflicts around the world dragging on for longer periods, a safe return home is a distant hope for

REFUGEE RIGHTS AND WRONGS

One challenge for Syrian refugees is that their primary host countries have weak protections in place for refugees. Turkey has signed both the 1951 Refugee Convention and its 1967 Protocol. However, it retains the geographical restriction that limits refugee status to European refugees. This means that refugee rights and protections are not seen as applying to people from countries outside of Europe, such as Syria. Jordan and Lebanon have not signed either document. But even countries that fully recognize refugee rights are guilty of violating them. In 2016, Amnesty International accused several European countries, including Germany and England, of forcing thousands of Afghan refugees to return home at a time of skyrocketing civilian casualties. This is a breach of the right of non-refoulement—the right of refugees not to be forcibly returned to a situation of danger. Australia has also come under fire for its policy of intercepting asylum seekers' boats and pushing them back to sea.

many refugees. In 2015, the lowest number of refugees returned home since 1983. Some 60 percent of refugees today have been displaced from their homes for more than five years. The average refugee will be displaced for more than ten years.[11]

A tiny fraction of the world's refugees find a way out through resettlement. This is a process of transferring refugees from the asylum country where they are sheltering to a third country that has agreed to admit them and allow them to permanently settle. Currently, just 37 countries offer resettlement places for refugees. And fewer than 200,000 refugees were resettled around the world in 2016. That's less than 1 percent.[12]

Those who are not among the lucky few all too often end up like Ali, a 38-year-old refugee from Syria. Ali fled to Jordan with his family in 2011. Expecting the conflict in Syria to be short lived, he thought he would be able to return home soon. Instead, he has been trapped in limbo for years. In Jordan, Ali isn't allowed to get a work permit. His savings have been depleted. The small stipend he receives from aid agencies has been cut in half. Unable to work legally, Ali collects discarded soda cans for recycling. He scavenges from midnight to dawn, making the equivalent of about eight dollars a night. It is far from enough to support his family of ten, including a handicapped son.

Like Jordan, most of the world's top refugee-hosting countries place significant restrictions on refugees. Many either deny refugees the right

HOW DOES RESETTLEMENT WORK?

Every year, the UNHCR registers millions of asylum seekers around the world. Out of that number, it identifies certain people who are considered especially vulnerable. These include survivors of torture, victims of sexual violence, targets of political persecution, people with serious medical conditions, and single mothers with multiple children. These especially vulnerable refugees are considered candidates for resettlement abroad. However, before they can be referred for overseas settlement, they must undergo extensive UNHCR screenings, including background checks, in-depth interviews, and biometric tests such as fingerprint or retinal scans. Of those who are referred for resettlement, only a tiny fraction are actually resettled.

to work legally or place significant barriers to employment. Many block any path to citizenship or even permanent residency. Educational opportunities for refugee children are limited. According to Human Rights Watch, a human rights nonprofit group, only one-half of all school-aged Syrian children in Turkey, Lebanon, and Jordan are in school. In Ethiopia, things are even worse. Only a small percentage of refugee children in Ethiopia attend school, according to Amnesty International. Such conditions condemn refugees to a life on the margins.

MORE TO THE
STORY

CHILDREN AT WORK

Denied the right to work legally, many Syrian refugees in Turkey, Lebanon, and Jordan resort to working on the black market, where they are exploited for their cheap labor. The situation has also caused a troubling epidemic of child labor. Children are less likely to be arrested for working illegally. As a result, many desperate refugee families resort to sending their children out to work. Experts estimate that thousands of Syrian child refugees in Turkey, Lebanon, and Jordan are working long hours in menial jobs—often for the equivalent of less than three dollars per day.

One of these workers is 16 year old Shrivan. He fled to Turkey in 2013 when his neighborhood in Aleppo, Syria, was destroyed by heavy shelling. Back home, Shrivan was one of the top students in his class. In Turkey, he has had to give up his education to help his family make ends meet. He was only 13 years old when he began working 12-hour shifts in a fabric factory.

FROM THE
HEADLINES

THE WORLD'S TOP REFUGEE HOSTS

Refugee crises occur in countries experiencing severe violence and warfare or extreme political instability. These countries are more likely to be in poor regions of the world. Since refugees typically flee to the first relatively safe country they can get to, that means a disproportionate share of the burden is falling on the world's poorer nations. Together, the ten countries with the greatest number of refugees account for only 2.5 percent of the world's income. The only wealthy Western nation on the list of top refugee hosts in 2016 was Germany. As a whole, Europe has only 11 percent of the world's refugees but 20 percent of the world's income. The United States accounts for 25 percent of global income but hosts only 1 percent of the world's refugees.[13]

TOP HOST COUNTRIES
FOR REFUGEES IN 2016[22]

TURKEY 2.8 Million

GERMANY 669,408

IRAN 979,435

LEBANON 1 Million

JORDAN 685,178

PAKISTAN 1.3 Million

DEMOCRATIC REPUBLIC OF THE CONGO 451,947

ETHIOPIA 791,616

KENYA 451,077

UGANDA 940,815

CHAPTER SIX

THE EUROPEAN
REFUGEE
CRISIS

Starting around 2014, more and more refugees began making their way to Europe. By 2015, the numbers had reached historic proportions. Several factors were behind the sudden surge. As violence in Syria continued to escalate, more Syrians were forced to flee. Syria's overburdened neighbors began making it more difficult for refugees to enter. Meanwhile, Syrian refugees who were already in neighboring countries found life becoming more unlivable as their host countries buckled under the strain and international assistance dried up. Worsening

Refugees register themselves at the Reception and Identification Center in Fylakio, Greece.

violence in Libya and Egypt made those countries increasingly dangerous for refugees, too.

These grim realities left many refugees desperate to seek a brighter future in wealthier, safer Europe—even if it meant risking their lives. All too often, dangerous journeys by sea or land were the only routes to Europe. "If people were receiving enough assistance and were able to have a somewhat stable life where they are, they would not make that decision," explains Dina El-Kassaby of the UN World Food Programme. "But unfortunately, some people are pushed to the edge."[1]

In 2015, an aid worker helped Syrian refugee children off a boat that arrived on the Greek island Lesbos.

One of those pushed to the edge was Mounib Zakiya, a Syrian refugee who fled to Jordan in 2012. In Jordan, the former real estate agent's family of nine survived on the equivalent of nine dollars a day. That came in the form of a monthly stipend from the UN World Food Programme. However, in 2015, even that lifeline was cut. No longer able to pay for food, medicine, or rent, Zakiya made up his mind to try to get his family to Europe, whatever the risks.

A MASS EXODUS

Huge numbers of other refugees from Syria made the same decision. They were joined by increasing numbers of refugees escaping worsening conflicts elsewhere in the world. The result was the largest influx ever of refugees and migrants from outside of Europe. In 2014, there were hundreds of thousands of arrivals within the EU. In 2015, the number jumped to more than one million. By comparison, the number in 2012 had been just 72,000.[2]

By September 2015, an average of 4,500 people a day were arriving on the Greek islands in the Aegean Sea—the main entry points for refugees journeying through Turkey. In the beginning of October, the number of refugees exploded to 7,000 a day.[3] With beds for only a couple thousand people, the island of Lesbos struggled to keep up with 10,000 people at a time.[4] A significant number of refugees came from Somalia, Afghanistan, Iraq, and Eritrea.

In the same period of time, Italy was seeing thousands of arrivals each day. These asylum seekers reached Italy by crossing the Mediterranean Sea from Libya and Egypt on the North African coast. About one-third of those making the dangerous sea crossing were Syrian refugees. Others came mainly from sub-Saharan African countries including Eritrea, Nigeria, Somalia, Sudan, and South Sudan.

Altogether, more than 850,000 migrants and refugees entered Greece in 2015. More than 150,000 came through Italy.[5] Overall, the majority of the people reaching Europe's shores came from the world's top ten refugee-producing countries.

But although Greece and Italy were the main migration hubs, few asylum seekers wanted to stay there. These southern European countries are among Europe's poorer nations. Greece in particular has been in the grip of an economic crisis since 2007, with skyrocketing rates of unemployment and poverty. Most asylum seekers hoped to ultimately make their way to the wealthier countries of northern Europe, including Germany and Sweden. These countries offer more protection and support for asylum seekers and a more welcoming environment. However, getting there requires a long trek over land across multiple borders.

ENTERING EUROPE

The massive flow of people into Europe at this time was

FLEEING HOME ALONE

Almost one-half of the asylum seekers coming through Greece since 2015 have been children. A growing number have been unaccompanied minors—children younger than 18 years who are traveling without a responsible adult. In 2015, there were more than 88,000 asylum applications by unaccompanied minors in Europe. That was four times the number reported in 2014. Altogether, almost one out of every four refugee children arriving in Europe in 2015 was an unaccompanied minor.[7] Some were as young as six. All children need special protection in situations of danger and insecurity. Children traveling alone are especially vulnerable to harm. They are at increased risk of falling victim to violence, abuse, and exploitation. Claude Moraes, the chair of the European Parliament's Justice and Home Affairs Committee, has warned of awful levels of child abuse in unsafe refugee camps in Greece and Italy.

unprecedented. Politicians reacted in alarm. International headlines dubbed the situation a European refugee crisis. But experts say that the cause of the crisis was not the sudden influx of people seeking shelter in Europe. Instead, the crisis was caused by Europe's failure to adequately respond to the situation.

One million refugees may be unprecedented for Europe. But that number represents just a tiny fraction of the EU's total population. Poorer regions of the world are absorbing a much greater number—both in absolute terms and in proportion to their populations. "The European refugee crisis was not a crisis of numbers; it was a crisis of politics," said Betts. "Twenty-eight EU member states should have been able to manage an influx of 1 million refugees—a number less than, say, Lebanon or Uganda host by themselves."[8]

Instead, the continent degenerated into chaos, experts such as Betts say. Responses to the influx differed country by country, with no consistent, unified approach in place. Policies changed day by day, disrupting refugees who were already in transit. Betts and Collier explained that the governments in the EU began to panic. Countries across

The fence between Hungary and Serbia to keep refugees out was built in 2015.

the continent tightened their borders and blocked safe and legal routes to asylum. Hungary built a razor wire fence to keep asylum seekers out and deployed armed forces around its border. Bulgaria, Slovenia, Macedonia, and Austria followed suit. Going to the other extreme, Germany declared an open-door policy for Syrian refugees at the end of August 2015.

Germany's open-door policy meant that it would accept any refugees from Syria, regardless of where they had first entered the continent. This encouraged even greater numbers of desperate Syrians to set out for European shores. However, within a few months,

German chancellor Angela Merkel backpedaled on her pledge. As would-be asylum seekers flooded into German towns, Merkel faced a political backlash. The country began tightening controls on its borders, reversing its open-door policy.

SHARING THE BURDEN?

As the influx of asylum seekers swelled, Greece and Italy struggled to cope. EU leaders met in September 2015 to talk about how to relieve the pressure. Eventually they agreed to a quota system. According to the plan, 120,000 asylum seekers would be relocated from Greece and Italy to other countries throughout the rest of Europe.[9] The goal was to spread out the number of asylum seekers in a more sustainable way. However, according to journalist Patrick Kingsley, the plan was an inadequate response. Compared with the massive numbers streaming in, 120,000 amounted to a mere drop in the bucket. Moreover, the agreement remained voluntary—in other words, it was up to individual countries to decide whether to live up to their end of the bargain. Most ignored it, and the agreement went unenforced. A year later, just a couple thousand refugees had been relocated.

DEADLY CONSEQUENCES

In the meantime, tens of thousands of asylum seekers remained in Greece and Italy, waiting in overcrowded, squalid conditions for their asylum claims to be processed. Thousands were left stranded at blocked border crossings, forced to camp out in harsh weather with little food. And thousands continued to lose their lives trying to make it out of war zones on flimsy inflatable rafts.

An estimated 3,500 people died in 2014 trying to make it to Europe.[10] That number rose to more than 3,700 in 2015. In 2016, the death toll surpassed 5,000. "That means that, on average, 14 people have died every single day this year in the Mediterranean trying to find safety or a better life in Europe," UNHCR spokesman William Spindler says.[11]

These tragedies are the result of the deadly dilemma refugees face. Asylum seekers have to reach Europe in order to claim asylum there. But many do not have the documents they need to get a normal travel visa so that they can travel by safe and legal routes. As a result, many people resort to unsafe routes operated by smugglers, including perilous sea journeys in overcrowded, rickety boats.

EVERYDAY HEROES

Human rights groups have accused Europe of inhumane policies that put refugees' lives at risk. However, many ordinary citizens responded with great heroism and humanity to the plight of refugees washing up on their shores. One of these people was Antonis Deligiorgis, a 34-year-old Greek army sergeant who single-handedly rescued more than a dozen people from a shipwrecked boat off the island of Rhodes. The boat, carrying Syrian and Eritrean asylum seekers, was on its way to Rhodes from the Turkish coast. Close to shore, it hit rocks and fell apart. Deligiorgis, who was sitting at a seafront café at the time, instantly ran to the beach and leaped into the sea to help. One of the women he rescued, an Eritrean woman named Elizabeth, was heavily pregnant. A few days later, she gave birth to a son. She named him Antonis George in honor of her rescuer.

A SYMBOL OF THE CRISIS

Three-year-old Alan Kurdi and his family were originally from Kobanî, a city in northern Syria. Like most of the area's residents, they were Kurds, an ethnic minority that faces discrimination under the Syrian government. They lived an ordinary life in a working-class neighborhood. His father, Abdullah, was a barber. His mother, Rehanna, worked as a seamstress. In the summers, they tended the family's olive groves.

However, by 2014, the escalating civil war in Syria had turned their lives upside down. In the Kobanî region, village after village fell under attack by ISIS. Locked in battle between ISIS militants and Kurdish rebel forces, the area was assailed by tanks, rockets, and artillery. ISIS terrorized civilians with mass killings, abductions, and brutal acts of torture and rape. In turn, United States–led coalition forces responded with air strikes to curb ISIS's advance.

Things got so dangerous that the family fled to neighboring Turkey in late 2014. However, like most Syrians in Turkey, Abdullah and Rehanna were not able to get work

When fleeing their homes, people often seek refuge in neighboring countries. In 2018, some people fled the Democratic Republic of the Congo and sought refuge in Uganda.

permits. And like many ethnic minorities in Syria, the Kurds had been denied passports by their own government back home. Without the right to work legally in Turkey, the family was stuck in poverty. Without passports, they could not get an exit visa to seek asylum in another country—even though Abdullah's sister in Canada was willing to sponsor her brother and his family.

In desperation, Abdullah borrowed money from his sister to pay a smuggler. For the equivalent of a few thousand dollars, the smuggler would ferry them across the Aegean Sea to the Greek island of Kos. Though the island was just a few miles away, the crossing could be rough. The smuggler promised a sturdy, motorized boat. Instead, when the family arrived at the port on September 2, 2015, they found a small rubber raft waiting for them.

A few minutes after setting out, the flimsy raft overturned in the choppy waves. Alan, his mother, and his five-year-old brother Ghalib drowned, along with several other passengers.

"OF COURSE WE WERE AFRAID OF DROWNING, BUT THE TURKISH SMUGGLER SAID IT WAS GOING TO BE A YACHT."[12]

—ABDULLAH KURDI, FATHER OF THREE-YEAR-OLD ALAN KURDI, WHO DROWNED EN ROUTE TO EUROPE ON SEPTEMBER 2, 2015

Abdullah was the only family member who survived. Later, a journalist snapped a photo of Alan's small body washed up on the shore, lying facedown in the sand. The heart-wrenching image was shared around the world—a tragic symbol of the plight of countless refugees.

Many boats that refugees travel on are not safe.

FROM THE HEADLINES

A CONTROVERSIAL DEAL

In 2016, Europe saw a dramatic decrease in asylum seekers reaching its shores by sea. Arrivals dropped from more than one million in 2015 to a couple hundred thousand in 2016. In large part, the decrease was due to a controversial deal between the EU and Turkey made in March of that year. In exchange for billions of dollars, Turkey agreed to take back asylum seekers who had entered the EU through irregular channels—in other words, people who entered the EU without applying for asylum beforehand. This would include people like Alan Kurdi and his family members, who were unable to go through regular channels because they lacked proper travel documents.

For every irregular asylum seeker Turkey took back, the EU agreed to resettle one qualifying Syrian refugee from Turkey. Critics argue that Turkey is not a safe place for refugees and that forcibly returning asylum seekers to Turkey is unethical. It also violates international law, they say. "There is no such thing as an illegal asylum seeker," journalist Charlotte McDonald-Gibson said. "The UN convention on refugees allows a person fleeing conflict to enter a country without the required paperwork."[13]

The number of refugees coming into Europe by sea decreased between 2015 and 2016.

REFUGEES COMING
INTO EUROPE BY SEA
IN 2015 AND 2016[14]

2015 TOTAL SEA ARRIVALS TO ITALY AND GREECE: 1,010,565

ITALY
153,842

GREECE
856,723

TURKEY

SICILY

TUNISIA

LIBYA

EGYPT

2016 TOTAL SEA ARRIVALS TO ITALY AND GREECE: 354,886

ITALY
115,068

GREECE
163,744

TURKEY

SICILY

TUNISIA

LIBYA

EGYPT

CHAPTER SEVEN

UNITED STATES
AND REFUGEES

Author Laurie Penny says, "Given the right papers and a basic amount of help at the border, the children of Syrian and Afghanistan and Eritrea could be starting new lives in less than a day." Instead, hundreds of thousands of refugees have been forced to endure long, perilous ordeals—dangerous boat crossings, exhausting journeys on foot from one end of Europe to the other, and months inside filthy refugee reception centers. The refugee crisis is a "battle for the soul of Europe," she writes in a column for the *New Statesman*.[1]

But the problem isn't Europe's alone. The United States bears some of the responsibility too, *New York Times* journalist Patrick Kingsley says. "This crisis is billed

Protesters showed their support for refugees at the Portland, Oregon, International Airport in 2018.

as a European one, but it is also the result of America's failure to resettle a meaningful number of Syrian refugees and so lessen the burden on the Middle East and Europe," he explains in his book *The New Odyssey: The Story of Europe's Refugee Crisis.*[2]

A LOW NUMBER

By the time three-year-old Alan's drowned body washed to shore in September 2015, the United States had taken in fewer than 1,500 Syrian refugees since the beginning of the war. Under pressure to do more, President Barack

Baraa Haj Khalaf, *left*, and her child were greeted by Khalaf's brother and mother at O'Hare International Airport in Illinois in 2017. Khalaf lived in a refugee camp in Turkey for five years.

Obama pledged to take in 10,000 Syrian refugees in the next year.[3]

Given the scope of the crisis, this was still a low number, said Eleanor Acer of Human Rights First, a New York–based nonprofit. In the end, the United States surpassed that benchmark, resettling 15,479 Syrian refugees in 2016.[4] However, to put that number into perspective, that is roughly the number of asylum seekers Greek officials on the island of Lesbos registered in a single day in September 2015.

The number of Syrian refugees the United States has admitted is not just low in relation to the scale of the crisis. It is also low in relation to the United States' past responses to refugee crises around the world. After the Vietnam War (1955–1975), 1.3 million refugees from Southeast Asia were in need of resettlement. The United States gave sanctuary to 800,000 of them.[5] Some 120,000 Cuban asylum seekers found refuge in the United States in 1980, including 80,000 people who were admitted in a single month.[6] And hundreds of thousands of refugees fleeing conflicts in the Balkans region in southeastern Europe found homes in the United States in the 1990s. Overall, the United States has resettled millions of refugees since 1980—more than any other country.

However, the general trend since the mid-2010s represents a break with past tradition. Even as the refugee population worldwide grows to record levels, the number admitted by the United States has been shrinking. That trend has accelerated sharply under President Donald Trump.

IMMIGRANTS AND REFUGEES

The United States is known as a nation of immigrants. Many of the country's immigrants have been refugees—those fleeing political and religious persecution. For most of its history, the United States didn't differentiate between immigrants and refugees. The 1948 Displaced Persons Act was the first step toward enshrining that distinction in law. It was created to deal with a wave of refugees from Europe after World War II. The Refugee Act of 1980 created the first comprehensive set of rules for refugee admissions. While US refugee policy largely mirrors the terms set out in the 1951 UN Refugee Convention, there are some differences. For example, US law does not require asylum seekers to be outside their country of origin when they apply for refugee status. They can apply while still in their own country and wait from home for their status to be determined.

LOWERING THE CEILING AND SHUTTING THE DOOR ON REFUGEES

Every year, the White House sets a ceiling, or maximum number, for how many refugees are resettled in the country. The number fluctuates from year to year, typically in response to the size of the refugee population worldwide. In the early 1980s, the ceiling was as high as 231,000. Under the George W. Bush and Obama administrations, the number averaged between 70,000 and 80,000.[7]

At the end of his term, Obama bumped the ceiling up to 110,000 for 2017—a nod to the world's growing refugee crisis. The Trump administration slashed that number to 50,000—the lowest ever.[8] In a letter to the White House, a bipartisan group of 34 US senators called that number "insufficient when compared to the millions of people who have been forced to flee their countries." They urged Trump to raise the ceiling significantly for the next year. "The current global humanitarian crisis requires strong American leadership," they wrote. "Failing to do our part to protect the victims of this global crisis undermines U.S. leadership, diplomacy, and national security."[9] Instead, the Trump administration dropped the ceiling even lower, setting an annual cap of 45,000 refugees for 2018.[10]

While these annual caps are historically low, the actual

"THE THREAT OF A DRASTICALLY LOW CEILING ON REFUGEE ARRIVALS IN THE U.S. IS CONTRARY TO AMERICAN VALUES AND THE SPIRIT OF GENEROSITY IN AMERICAN CHURCHES AND COMMUNITIES."[11]

—LINDA HARTKE, PRESIDENT OF LUTHERAN IMMIGRATION AND REFUGEE SERVICE

numbers admitted have been even lower. In 2017, the United States accepted only 29,022 refugees from around the world.[12] The year 2018 was on track to be a record-low year for refugee admissions. Just 11 Syrian refugees were resettled in the first three months of 2018. By comparison, during the same three-month period in 2016, the number was 790. "I think [the Trump administration] closed the front door to America," says Becca Heller, a member of the New York–based International Refugee Assistance Project.[13]

REGIONAL CEILINGS

In addition to an overall cap on refugee admissions from all countries, the Trump administration issued caps for the maximum number of refugees the United States will accept from specific regions. For 2018, those caps were set at no more than 19,000 refugees from Africa, 17,500 from the Middle East and South Asia, 5,000 from East Asia, 2,000 from Europe and central Asia, and 1,500 from Latin America and the Caribbean. In previous years, presidents have included what is known as an "unallocated reserve" quota.[14] This allows for admitting extra numbers of refugees beyond the specified quota. That allows leeway to respond to an unexpected surge in refugees—as would happen when there is an unforeseen crisis or suddenly worsening conflict. The Trump administration did not include that provision in its 2018 refugee admissions cap.

TRUMP'S TRAVEL BAN

Refugee admissions have slowed to a crawl, experts say, because of Trump administration policies that have made it more difficult for refugees to enter the country. Shortly after taking office in

January 2017, Trump issued a travel ban targeting citizens from seven majority-Muslim nations, namely Iraq, Syria, Iran, Libya, Somalia, Sudan, and Yemen. People from these countries were temporarily blocked from entering the United States. The ban also indefinitely barred Syrian refugees from admission and temporarily halted refugee admissions from anywhere in the world.

Federal courts struck down the ban, arguing that the restrictions were unconstitutional. However, in the meantime, the ban had devastating effects on many refugees. One of these was Momina Hassan Aden, a 38-year-old refugee from Somalia. After fleeing her war-torn country in 2013, Aden took shelter in a refugee camp in northwestern Kenya.

FAMILIES STUCK

Many refugee families have been caught in the crosshairs of Trump's travel ban. Mohamed Chaghlil's family is one of them. The 35-year-old and his parents escaped the Syrian civil war in December 2012, fleeing to Jordan. From there, they applied to settle in the United States. By the fall of 2016, Chaghlil was finally approved for travel to the United States. In the meantime, however, his father had died. Since his mother's marital status had now changed, she had to go through checks on her application again. Chaghlil decided to go ahead with his travel plans. He arrived in his new hometown of New Haven, Connecticut, shortly before Trump took office. He expected his mother to join him soon. Instead, Trump's travel ban turned their plans upside down. As of April 2018, Chaghlil's elderly mother was still waiting to be reunited with her son.

In 2018, travel ban protesters voiced their disapproval outside the Supreme Court.

The sprawling camp had been her home for four years. However, she was unable to get the kind of care she needed for a serious medical condition. She was accepted for resettlement in the United States and had been cleared for travel when Trump's ban took effect. As a result, her resettlement process was put on hold indefinitely.

In June 2018, the US Supreme Court upheld Trump's revised version of the travel ban, which blocks travelers from Iran, Libya, North Korea, Somalia, Syria, Venezuela, and Yemen from entering the United States. This version does not restrict refugee admissions. However, it adds new vetting requirements to an already rigorous screening process. Refugee advocates say that these added requirements will slow down the refugee admissions process and make it harder for vulnerable people to make it into the United States.

Central American and Mexican asylum seekers also faced struggles getting into the United States in 2018. The Trump administration had a zero tolerance immigration policy for people who came to the United States without official documentation. At the US–Mexico border, government officials charged asylum seekers with a crime for entering the United States without permission. After they were charged with a crime, the asylum seekers were sent to jail. Thousands of children were separated from their parents under this policy.

The public and various politicians expressed outrage over Trump's policy, causing Trump to sign an executive order in June 2018 to stop the policy of separating children and parents. That same month, a federal judge declared that children had to be reunited with their families by July 26, and the majority of children were.

CHAPTER EIGHT

REFUGEES AND
TERRORISM

The White House argues that Trump's travel ban and his restrictions on refugees are needed to protect the country. "The security and safety of the American people is our chief concern," one senior government official said about the president's decision to slash refugee admissions to a historic low.[1] Trump and his supporters worry that taking in more refugees could lead to more terrorism and crime. They argue that tougher vetting is needed to weed out possible extremists. Similarly, they maintain that the travel ban is justified because citizens from the targeted nations could be a security threat to the United States.

Some Muslim Americans responded to Trump's travel ban by attending "pray-ins."

ISLAMOPHOBIA AND THE BACKLASH AGAINST REFUGEES

Trump's critics argue that his policies are fueled by Islamophobia, or anti-Muslim bias. In recent decades, escalating conflicts in the Middle East have created increasing numbers of refugees from majority-Muslim nations. At the same time, hostility in the United States toward Muslim immigrants and refugees has been on the rise since the terrorist attacks of September 11, 2001.

That hostility started turning against Syrian refugees in particular after deadly terrorist attacks in Paris, France. In November 2015, a series of mass shootings and suicide bombings killed and wounded hundreds of people in the French capital. When a Syrian passport was found by the body of one of the suicide bombers, a wave of panic ensued. People assumed that the suicide bomber was a Syrian refugee. "Overnight, the global good will toward refugees that had been building all but vanished," journalist Eliza Griswold reports. "Suddenly, the images of hundreds of thousands of refugees heading north inspired not empathy but alarm."[2]

Experts later determined that the passport was fake. The chaos of Europe's response to the refugee crisis had created a thriving black market in forged passports. The suicide bomber had likely exploited that chaos to mask his identity, possibly because he was on a terrorist watch list. All the Paris attackers who were identified were in fact European nationals, not refugees, officials confirmed.

"WE HAVE SEEN ENOUGH VIOLENCE AND BLOODSHED. WE CAME HERE TO ESCAPE THE WAR, NOT TO START ONE."[4]

—NSREEN, A SYRIAN REFUGEE WHO WAS RESETTLED IN CHARLOTTESVILLE, VIRGINIA

Despite these findings, the incident unleashed a backlash against Syrian refugees in both the United States and Europe. Politicians vowed to crack down on asylum seekers and to tighten borders. In the United States, the majority of US governors said they would refuse to let any Syrian refugees into their states. "I will do everything humanly possible to stop any plans from the Obama Administration to put Syrian refugees in Mississippi," Governor Phil Bryant said. "The policy of bringing these individuals into the country is not only misguided, it is extremely dangerous."[3]

Wisconsin governor Scott Walker said that terrorists could try to take advantage of the refugee resettlement program to enter the country. "There may be those who will try to take advantage of the generosity of our country and the ability to move freely within our borders through this federal resettlement program, and we must ensure we are doing all we can to safeguard the security of Americans."[5]

TERRORISM IN EUROPE

Europe and the United States are in very different positions when it comes to Syrian refugees. Those refugees who are resettled in the United States have already been thoroughly screened before they set foot in the country. By contrast, Syrian asylum seekers show up on Europe's doorstep before they have been vetted. Nonetheless, the actual terrorist threat from Syrian refugees is very low even in Europe, according to Georgetown University professor Daniel L. Byman. However, if the refugee crisis is handled poorly, the potential risks of a future problem could be high, he says. According to Byman, European-born Islamic extremists—such as the Paris attackers—largely grew up in marginalized communities where it was hard for immigrants to integrate into society. That is how they became radicalized. If Europe fails to help its growing Syrian refugee community integrate into society, then it may be breeding a new generation of extremists, Byman warns.

VICTIMS OF TERRORISM, NOT TERRORISTS

Critics argue that this type of response is wrongheaded. Refugees undergoing resettlement in the United States are already more thoroughly vetted than any other travelers. And they are far more likely to be victims of terrorism than terrorists themselves, the data shows.

Since 2001, the United States has admitted close to 900,000 refugees. According to Alex Nowrasteh, an immigration expert at the Cato Institute, only three refugees have been convicted of attempted terrorism. None of these attempts were successful, and none were carried out on US soil. The terrorist threat posed by refugees in the United States is so small that Nowrasteh puts the odds of dying at the hands of a refugee at just one in 3.64 billion.[6] In fact, very few attacks on US soil are linked to any foreign nationals at all. The majority of extremist attacks in the United States are committed by homegrown white supremacist groups and other far-right extremists.

But the Trump administration's policies aren't just unnecessary, according to his critics. They are also counterproductive. Harsh policies against refugees are a promotional gift and a recruiting tool for radical Islamic terrorist groups. These groups have a vested interest in painting the United States—and the West in general—as barbaric and cruel. Slamming the door on vulnerable

Trump's travel ban faced an uphill legal battle in various courts but was ultimately upheld by the Supreme Court.

people from war-torn nations provides fodder for their cause, refugee advocates say.

A slew of national security and foreign policy experts has also criticized Trump's travel ban on similar grounds. For example, James Clapper, former director of National Intelligence, argues that the ban alienates Muslims around the world and so makes it harder to gather credible intelligence about real security threats. "It's unnecessary, at odds with the Constitution, and ultimately counterproductive because it makes Americans less safe rather than more," he wrote in an opinion article for CNN.[7] More than 130 former defense and foreign policy officials echoed that idea in a letter delivered to the White House in March 2017. The ban "will send a message that reinforces the propaganda of ISIS and other extremist groups, that falsely claim the United States is at war with Islam," the letter said. "Welcoming Muslim refugees and travelers, by contrast, exposes the lies of terrorists and counters their warped vision."[8]

RISING TO THE CHALLENGE

Ultimately, nobody argues that security and terrorism are not legitimate concerns. And nobody denies that proper screening is important. However, refugee advocates say that it is wrong to demonize refugees based on unfounded fears. Refugees are among the world's most vulnerable people. They have fled horrific situations of war and persecution. Many of them have suffered terribly at the hands of terrorists. As the IRC's David Miliband says, "It

REFUGEES WELCOME

US policies have made it harder for refugees to enter the United States, but plenty of ordinary Americans are working hard to show refugees that they are welcome. One of them is Pittsburgh, Pennsylvania, resident Sloane Davidson. She is the founder of Hello Neighbor. This is a mentorship program that matches recently arrived refugee families with American families to help them transition to their lives in a new country. In Los Angeles, California, Miry Whitehill is also helping refugees settle in their new communities. When Whitehill heard about a family of Syrian refugees who needed baby gear for their seven-month-old, the 32-year-old mom set up an organization called Miry's List. It publishes wish lists of items that refugee families urgently need and uses crowdsourcing and social media to connect the families with donors. In a year and a half, Miry's List helped hundreds of refugee families all around the country.

Many refugees are simply looking for a safe place to call home.

is wrong to make victims of terror pay twice over for the actions of terrorists, first when they lose everything in war or conflict, then by denying them a chance to restart their lives."[9]

As long as conflicts continue to erupt around the world, there will continue to be large numbers of refugees forced to flee their homelands. The rest of the world will have to rise up to the challenge. That requires finding ways that are both effective and humane to deal with the biggest refugee crisis since World War II. "Refugees and displaced people have lost everything," Miliband says. "But the refugee crisis is not just about 'them'; it is also about 'us'—what we, living in far greater comfort, stand for and how we see our place in the world. It is a test of our character, not just our policies. Pass the test, and we rescue ourselves and our values as well as refugees and their lives."[10]

AN ASSET, NOT A THREAT

Welcoming refugees does more than help vulnerable people get on their feet again. It also benefits society. That's the conclusion of a growing number of studies. Michael Clemens of the Center for Global Development, a think tank based in Washington, DC, says that he hasn't seen any legitimate research showing that refugees aren't a good investment. Studies show that refugees create jobs and boost the economy. According to Clemens, this is because they are more likely than other groups to start businesses. Beyond their economic impact, refugees also enrich society in other important ways. Some even transform the world—such as Soviet Union refugee Sergey Brin, a cofounder of Google.

ESSENTIAL
FACTS

MAJOR EVENTS

- At the end of World War II, millions of refugees were displaced from their homes. The international community responded to the horrors of the war by creating protections for human rights and the rights of refugees specifically.

- In March 2011, protests broke out in Syria. Syrian president Bashar al-Assad responded with a brutal crackdown. Soon, the situation escalated into a full-blown civil war.

- Starting around 2014, increased numbers of refugees from Syria and elsewhere began crossing to Europe.

- The Trump administration slashed the refugee admissions ceiling to 50,000 for 2017 and 45,000 for 2018—a record low.

KEY PLAYERS

- On September 2, 2015, three-year-old Alan Kurdi, a Syrian refugee, drowned on the way to Greece. A photo of his body gained widespread attention, causing a surge of sympathy for the plight of Syrian refugees.

- President Donald Trump took office in January 2017. Soon afterward, he issued a travel ban targeting majority-Muslim nations. In June 2018, the Supreme Court upheld a version of this travel ban.

IMPACT ON SOCIETY

As of 2016, 65.6 million people were forcibly displaced because of conflict, persecution, or human rights abuses around the globe. Almost 23 million of these people were refugees. The majority of these refugees are hosted by some of the world's poorest countries. Syria is the largest single source of refugees. Underfunded humanitarian-assistance programs struggle to keep up with the demand, and so do Syria's neighbors, which are hosting historically high numbers of refugees. Lack of funding means that the conditions in these host countries have deteriorated for many refugees.

QUOTE

"The rising tide of people forced to leave their homes because of conflict or persecution is one of the most challenging issues facing the world today."

—David Miliband, CEO, International Rescue Committee, 2017

GLOSSARY

ASYLUM

Protection given by a country to someone who has left his or her country as a political refugee.

AUTHORITARIAN

Describing a political system that concentrates power in the hands of a leader or small ruling elite and limits civil and political freedoms and rights.

BLACK MARKET

A collection of buyers and sellers trading illegally, often in banned substances.

DICTATORSHIP

A government ruled by a dictator, or someone who wields absolute power.

EXTREMIST

A person who has extreme or fanatical political or religious views and often advocates violence.

FUNDAMENTALIST

Having to do with a form of religion that strictly adheres to a literal interpretation of scripture.

GENOCIDE

The deliberate mass murder of a group of people.

MILITANT

An individual who is willing to aggressively support a cause.

RAMPANT

Widespread and uncontrolled.

SHRAPNEL

Small metal fragments that are flung into the air by an exploding shell or bomb, causing risk of injury or death to anyone nearby.

SQUALID

Extremely dirty.

VETTING

A careful screening or checking.

VISA

An official authorization permitting entry into and travel within a country.

ADDITIONAL
RESOURCES

SELECTED BIBLIOGRAPHY

Jie Zong and Jeanne Batalova. "Syrian Refugees in the United States." *MPI*, 12 Jan. 2017, migrationpolicy.org. Accessed 13 June 2018.

"Mediterranean Boat Capsizing: Deadliest Incident on Record." *UNHCR*, n.d., unhcr.org. Accessed 13 June 2018.

"Tackling the Global Refugee Crisis: From Shirking to Sharing Responsibility." *Amnesty International*, 30 Sept. 2016, amnesty.org. Accessed 13 June 2018.

FURTHER READINGS

Capek, Michael. *The Syrian Conflict*. Abdo, 2017.

Marsico, Katie. *ISIS*. Abdo, 2016.

ONLINE RESOURCES

Booklinks
NONFICTION NETWORK
FREE! ONLINE NONFICTION RESOURCES

To learn more about the refugee crisis, visit **abdobooklinks.com**. These links are routinely monitored and updated to provide the most current information available.

MORE INFORMATION

For more information on this subject, contact or visit the following organizations:

International Rescue Committee (IRC)
122 E. Forty-Second St.
New York, NY 10168-1289
212-551-3000
rescue.org
The IRC is a global nongovernmental organization that responds to humanitarian crises around the world, including refugee crises.

Refugee Council USA
1628 Sixteenth St. NW
Washington, DC 20009
202-319-2102
rcusa.org
Refugee Council USA is an advocacy group dedicated to refugee protection and resettlement.

SOURCE
NOTES

CHAPTER 1. DESPERATE JOURNEYS

1. "Mediterranean Boat Capsizing: Deadliest Incident on Record." *UNHCR*, 12 Apr. 2015, unhcr.org. Accessed 23 July 2018.

2. "Siva's Story, Indonesia." *UNHCR*, n.d., unhcr.org. Accessed 23 July 2018.

3. "European Commission Statement on Developments in the Mediterranean." *European Commission*, 19 Apr. 2015, europa.eu. Accessed 23 July 2018.

4. "Pope Urges World Action to Stop More Migrant Disasters." *Reuters*, 20 Apr. 2015, reuters.com. Accessed 23 July 2018.

5. "Migrant Crisis: Migration to Europe Explained in Seven Charts." *BBC News*, 4 Mar. 2016, bbc.com. Accessed 23 July 2018.

6. Patrick Kingsley. *The New Odyssey: The Story of Europe's Refugee Crisis.* Guardian Books, 2016. 291.

7. "Bay of Bengal 'Three Times More Deadly' Than Mediterranean for Migrants and Refugees." *UN News*, 23 Feb. 2016, news.un.org. Accessed 23 July 2018.

8. Tom Miles. "More Europe-Bound Migrants May Be Dying in Sahara Than at Sea: Report." *Reuters*, 15 July 2016, reuters.com. Accessed 23 July 2018.

9. "Mediterranean Boat Capsizing."

10. Mark Tran. "What You Need to Know About Eritrea." *Guardian*, 17 Aug. 2015, theguardian.com. Accessed 23 July 2018.

11. Kingsley, *The New Odyssey*, 50.

12. "Migrant Deaths along US–Mexico Border Remain High Despite Drop in Crossings." *UN*, 6 Feb. 2018, refugeesmigrants.un.org. Accessed 23 July 2018.

13. "Fatal Journeys." *International Organization for Migration*, n.d., publications.iom.int. Accessed 23 July 2018.

14. "Tackling the Global Refugee Crisis: From Shirking to Sharing Responsibility." *Amnesty International*, 30 Sept. 2016, amnestyusa.com. Accessed 23 July 2018.

15. Priyanka Boghani. "The 'Human Cost' of the EU's Response to the Refugee Crisis." *PBS*, 23 Jan. 2018, pbs.com. Accessed 23 July 2018.

16. "Refugees." *UNHCR*, 14 Mar. 2017, unhcr.org. Accessed 23 July 2018.

17. "Fatal Journeys."

CHAPTER 2. PROTECTING REFUGEES

1. Florence Looi. "Rohingya Refugees Seeking Shelter in Malaysia." *Al Jazeera*, 18 Apr. 2018, aljazeera.com. Accessed 23 July 2018.

2. Tonny Onyulo. "Uganda's Other Refugee Crisis: Discrimination Forces Many LGBT Ugandans to Seek Asylum." *USA Today*, 13 July 2017, usatoday.com. Accessed 23 July 2018.

3. "Worldwide Deaths in World War II." *National WWII Museum*, n.d., nationalww2museum.org. Accessed 23 July 2018.

4. "Introduction to the Holocaust." *United States Holocaust Memorial Museum*, n.d., ushmm.org. Accessed 23 July 2018.

5. Ishaan Tharoor. "What Americans Thought of Jewish Refugees on the Eve of World War II." *Washington Post*, 17 Nov. 2015, washingtonpost.com. Accessed 23 July 2018.

6. "Voyage of the St. Louis." *United States Holocaust Memorial Museum*, n.d., ushmm.org. Accessed 23 July 2018.

7. David Miliband. *Rescue: Refugees and the Political Crisis of Our Time*. Simon, 2017. 41.

8. Andrew Purvis. "Shahad Once Lived 'The Best Life,' Now, the Four-Year-Old Syrian Girl Needs Help." *UNHCR*, 7 June 2013, unhcr.org. Accessed 23 July 2018.

9. "Convention and Protocol Relating to the Status of Refugees." *UNHCR*, n.d., unhcr.org. Accessed 23 July 2018.

10. Charlotte McDonald-Gibson. *Cast Away: True Stories of Survival from Europe's Refugee Crisis*. New Press, 2016. 86.

11. "States Parties to the 1951 Convention Relating to the Status of Refugees and the 1967 Protocol." *UNHCR*, n.d., unhcr.org. Accessed 23 July 2018.

CHAPTER 3. A HUMANITARIAN EMERGENCY IN SYRIA

1. Lydia DePillis, et al. "A Visual Guide to 75 Years of Major Refugee Crises around the World." *Washington Post*, 21 Dec. 2015, washingtonpost.com. Accessed 23 July 2018.

2. "Remarks by António Guterres, United Nations High Commissioner for Refugees." *UNHCR*, 28 Oct. 2014, unhcr.org. Accessed 23 July 2018.

3. "Why Is There a War in Syria?" *BBC News*, 15 Mar. 2018, bbc.com. Accessed 23 July 2018.

4. Elizabeth G Ferris. *The Consequences of Chaos: Syria's Humanitarian Crisis and the Failure to Protect*. Brookings, 2016. 26.

5. Ferris, *The Consequences of Chaos*, 26.

6. "Delays in Access in Syria 'Will Mean Further Death,' Warns Top UN Relief Official." *UN News*, 29 June 2017, news.un.org. Accessed 23 July 2018.

7. "Syria Emergency." *UNHCR*, n.d., unhcr.org. Accessed 23 July 2018.

8. Marc Silver. "They Outnumber Refugees but Don't Often Make Headlines." *NPR*, 22 May 2017, npr.org. Accessed 23 July 2018.

9. "Shahad's Story, Lebanon." *UNHCR*, n.d., stories.unhcr.org. Accessed 23 July 2018.

10. "Syria War: Families Struggle to Survive in Eastern Ghouta, Under Siege." *BBC News*, 22 Feb. 2018, bbc.com. Accessed 23 July 2018.

11. Kareem Shaheen. "Pleas for Safe Passage for Civilians Trapped in Eastern Ghouta." *Guardian*, 17 Mar. 2018, theguardian.com. Accessed 23 July 2018.

12. "Syria War."

13. "7 Things You Need to Know about the Horror in Syria." *International Rescue Committee*, 9 Mar. 2018, rescue.org. Accessed 23 July 2018.

CHAPTER 4. GLOBAL CONFLICT

1. United Nations. "Syria Conflict at 5 Years." *UNHCR*, 15 Mar. 2016, unhcr.org. Accessed 23 July 2018.

2. David Miliband. *Rescue: Refugees and the Political Crisis of Our Time*. Simon, 2017. 40.

3. Beth Mitchneck, et al. "Europe's Forgotten Refugees." *Foreign Affairs*, 24 Aug. 2016, foreignaffairs.com. Accessed 23 July 2018.

4. Julian Coman. "On the Frontline of Europe's Forgotten War in Ukraine." *Guardian*, 12 Nov. 2017, theguardian.com. Accessed 23 July 2018.

5. "Over US$1.4 Billion Needed for South Sudan Refugees in 2017." *UNHCR*, 15 May 2017, unhcr.org. Accessed 23 July 2018.

6. Michelle Nichols. "U.N. Appeals for Help for Boko Haram Displaced; Nigeria a No-Show." *Reuters*, 25 Sept. 2015, reuters.com. Accessed 23 July 2018.

7. "Yemen: The Forgotten War." *Amnesty International*, n.d., amnesty.org. Accessed 23 July 2018.

8. Ewelina U. Uchab. "Yemen Became the World's Worst Humanitarian Crisis." *Forbes*, 5 Apr. 2018, forbes.com. Accessed 23 July 2018.

9. Saeed Kamali Dehghan. "Yemen's Food Crisis: 'We Die Either from the Bombing or the Hunger.'" *Guardian*, 8 Feb. 2017, theguardian.com. Accessed 23 July 2018.

10. Dehghan, "Yemen's Food Crisis."

11. Dehghan, "Yemen's Food Crisis."

12. "Under-Secretary-General and Emergency Relief Coordinator Stephen O'Brien Opening Statement." *Reliefweb*, 25 Sept. 2015, reliefweb.int. Accessed 23 July 2018.

13. Sebastian von Einsiedel, et al. "Civil War Trends and the Changing Nature of Armed Conflict." *Centre for Policy Research*, 25 Apr. 2017, cpr.unu.edu. Accessed 23 July 2018.

14. Emma Graham-Harrison. "The World Looks Away as Blood Flows in Burundi." *Guardian*, 10 Apr. 2016, theguardian.com. Accessed 23 July 2018.

15. Céline Schmitt. "Rescue on Lake Tanganyika." *UNHCR*, 26 May 2015, tracks.unhcr.org. Accessed 23 July 2018.

SOURCE NOTES
CONTINUED

16. Karen McVeigh. "'Now Is Not the Time': Violence Forces Refugees to Flee Afghanistan Again." *Guardian*, 15 Jan. 2018, theguardian.com. Accessed 23 July 2018.

17. Daniel Boffey. "Britain Accused of Unlawfully Deporting Afghan Asylum Seekers." *Guardian*, 4 Oct. 2017, theguardian.com. Accessed 23 July 2018.

CHAPTER 5. THE WORLDWIDE COMMUNITY

1. "Figures at a Glance." *UNHCR*, n.d., unhcr.org. Accessed 23 July 2018.

2. "With 1 Human in Every 113 Affected, Forced Displacement Hits Record High." *UNHCR*, 20 June 2016, unhcr.org. Accessed 23 July 2018.

3. "Syria's Refugee Crisis in Numbers." *Amnesty International*, 21 Dec. 2016, amnesty.ie. Accessed 23 July 2018.

4. Jie Zong and Jeanne Batalova. "Syrian Refugees in the United States." *Migration Policy*, 12 Jan. 2017, migrationpolicy.com. Accessed 24 July 2018.

5. "The Global Refugee Crisis." *Amnesty International*, 30 Sept. 2016, amnestyusa.com. Accessed 25 July 2018.

6. Esther Yu Hsi Lee. "Massive Funding Shortfall Puts South Sudanese Refugees on Brink of Death." *Think Progress*, 16 May 2017, thinkprogress.com. Accessed 24 July 2018.

7. "Lack of Funding Putting Help for Syrian Refugees and Hosts at Risk." *UNHCR*, 4 Apr. 2017, unhcr.org. Accessed 24 July 2018.

8. "UNHCR Warns of Worsening Displacement in Democratic Republic of the Congo." *UNHCR*, 24 Oct. 2017, unhcr.org. Accessed 24 July 2018.

9. Orla Guerin. "Aid Cuts Driving Jordan's Syrian Refugees to Risk All." *BBC News*, 11 Sept. 2015, bbc.com. Accessed 24 July 2018.

10. Alexander Betts. *Refuge: Rethinking Refugee Policy in a Changing World*. Oxford UP, 2017. 7.

11. David Miliband. *Rescue: Refugees and the Political Crisis of Our Time*. Simon, 2017. 26.

12. Miliband, *Rescue*, 101.

13. Miliband, *Rescue*, 28–29.

14. "Ranking of the Ten Largest Refugee-Hosting Countries, as of 2016." *Statista*, n.d., statista.com. Accessed 24 July 2018.

CHAPTER 6. THE EUROPEAN REFUGEE CRISIS

1. Orla Guerin. "Aid Cuts Driving Jordan's Syrian Refugees to Risk All." *BBC News*, 11 Sept. 2015, bbc.com. Accessed 24 July 2018.

2. Charlotte McDonald-Gibson. *Cast Away: True Stories of Survival from Europe's Refugee Crisis*. New Press, 2016. 88.

3. "Migrant Arrivals in Greece 'Surge' to 7,000 Daily." *BBC News*, 9 Oct. 2015, bbc.com. Accessed 24 July 2018.

4. McDonald-Gibson, *Cast Away*, 88.

5. "Europe Refugees & Migrants Emergency Response." *Reliefweb*, 29 Feb. 2016, reliefweb.int. Accessed 24 July 2018.

6. Patrick Kingsley. *The New Odyssey: The Story of Europe's Refugee Crisis*. Guardian Books, 2016. 5.

7. Khalid Koser. "Europe's Real Refugee Crisis: Unaccompanied Minors." *OUPblog*, 27 June 2016, blog.oup.com. Accessed 24 July 2018.

8. Noah Berlatsky. "The Western Belief That Refugees Are a Burden Is the Root Cause of Today's Global Crisis." *Quartz*, 28 Aug. 2017, qz.com. Accessed 24 July 2018.

9. "Migrant Crisis: EU Ministers Approve Disputed Quota Plan." *BBC News*, 22 Sept. 2015, bbc.com. Accessed 24 July 2018.

10. McDonald-Gibson, *Cast Away*, 177.

11. Ben Quinn. "Migrant Death Toll Passes 5,000 after Two Boats Capsize off Italy." *Guardian*, 23 Dec. 2016, theguardian.com. Accessed 24 July 2018.

12. Anne Barnard and Karam Shoumali. "Image of Drowned Syrian, Aylan Kurdi, 3, Brings Migrant Crisis into Focus." *New York Times*, 3 Sept. 2015, nytimes.com. Accessed 24 July 2018.

13. McDonald-Gibson, *Cast Away*, 138.

14. "Refugees & Migrants Sea Arrivals in Europe." *UNHCR*, Dec. 2016, data2.unhcr.org. Accessed 24 July 2018.

CHAPTER 7. UNITED STATES AND REFUGEES

1. Laurie Penny. "The Refugee Crisis Is a Battle for the Soul of Europe." *NewStatesman*, 23 Sept. 2015, newstatesman.com. Accessed 24 July 2018.

2. Patrick Kingsley. *The New Odyssey: The Story of Europe's Refugee Crisis*. Guardian Books, 2016. 7.

3. Gardiner Harris, et al. "Obama Increases Number of Syrian Refugees for U.S. Resettlement to 10,000." *New York Times*, 10 Sept. 2015, nytimes.com. Accessed 24 July 2018.

4. Deborah Amos. "The U.S. Has Accepted Only 11 Syrian Refugees This Year." *NPR*, 12 Apr. 2018, npr.org. Accessed 24 July 2018.

5. Max J. Rosenthal. "America Once Accepted 800,000 War Refugees. Is It Time to Do That Again? *Mother Jones*, 11 Sept. 2015, motherjones.com. Accessed 24 July 2018.

6. Harris et al. "Obama Increases Number of Syrian Refugees."

7. Christopher Ingraham. "The Incredible Shrinking Refugee Cap, in One Chart." *Washington Post*, 26 Sept. 2017, washingtonpost.com. Accessed 24 July 2018.

8. Ingraham, "The Incredible Shrinking Refugee Cap, in One Chart."

9. "Letter to Donald Trump." *Chris Murphy*, 25 Sept. 2017, murphy.senate.gov. Accessed 24 July 2018.

10. "White House Officially Issues Lowest Refugee Cap Ever." *VOA*, 29 Sept. 2017, voanews.com. Accessed 24 July 2018.

11. Julie Hirshfeld Davis and Miriam Jordan. "Trump Plans 45,000 Limit on Refugees Admitted to U.S." *New York Times*, 26 Sept. 2017, nytimes.com. Accessed 24 July 2018.

12. Alan Gomez. "Refugee Admissions to U.S. Plummet in 2017." *USA Today*, 3 Jan. 2018, usatoday.com. Accessed 24 July 2018.

13. Amos, "The U.S. Has Accepted Only 11 Syrian Refugees This Year."

14. Laura Koran. "Trump Administration Dramatically Scales Back Refugee Admissions." *CNN*, 27 Sept. 2017, cnn.com. Accessed 24 July 2018.

CHAPTER 8. REFUGEES AND TERRORISM

1. Laura Koran. "Trump Administration Dramatically Scales Back Refugee Admissions." *CNN*, 27 Sept. 2017, cnn.com. Accessed 24 July 2018.

2. Eliza Griswold. "Why Is It So Difficult for Syrian Refugees to Get into the U.S.?" *New York Times*, 24 Jan. 2016, nytimes.com. Accessed 24 July 2018.

3. Polly Mosendz. "In Light of Paris Attacks, 26 GOP Governors, One Democrat to Refuse Syrian Refugees." *Newsweek*, 16 Nov. 2015, newsweek.com. Accessed 24 July 2018.

4. Sabrina Siddiqui. "'A Hellish Nightmare:' How Trump's Travel Ban Hit a Syrian Refugee Family." *Guardian*, 4 Feb. 2018, theguardian.com. Accessed 24 July 2018.

5. Mosendz, "In Light of Paris Attacks, 26 GOP Governors, One Democrat to Refuse Syrian Refugees."

6. Alex Nowrasteh. "Terrorism and Immigration: A Risk Analysis." *Cato Institute*, 13 Sept. 2016, cato.org. Accessed 24 July 2018.

7. James Clapper, et al. "We've Worked on Stopping Terrorism. Trump's Travel Ban Fuels It." *CNN*, 23 Apr. 2018, cnn.com. Accessed 24 July 2018.

8. Nicholas Loffredo. "Trump Travel Ban Weakens National Security, Foreign Policy Experts Argue." *Newsweek*, 11 Mar. 2017, newsweek.com. Accessed 24 July 2018.

9. David Miliband. *Rescue: Refugees and the Political Crisis of Our Time*. Simon, 2017. 97.

10. Miliband, *Rescue*, 6.

INDEX

ABOUT THE
AUTHORS

DUCHESS HARRIS, JD, PHD

Professor Harris is the chair of the American Studies department at Macalester College and curator of the Duchess Harris Collection of ABDO books. She is the author and coauthor of recently released ABDO books including *Hidden Human Computers: The Black Women of NASA*, *Black Lives Matter*, and *Race and Policing*.

Before working with ABDO, she authored several other books on the topics of race, culture, and American history. She served as an associate editor for *Litigation News*, the American Bar Association Section of Litigation's quarterly flagship publication, and was the first editor in chief of *Law Raza*, an interactive online journal covering race and the law, published at William Mitchell College of Law. She has earned a PhD in American Studies from the University of Minnesota and a JD from William Mitchell College of Law.

ELISABETH HERSCHBACH

Elisabeth Herschbach is an editor, writer, and translator from Washington, DC.